Prologue

Hello, everyone Michael Lee Kilmartin is here to bring to you another new novel and inspiring story called "An Author is Born" and this story is about how I originated and pursued being a writer and an author. My life has had so many ups and downs, and yet some exciting new steps and developments in my lifetime. Some of my downs have been just stepping stones to my success. I want to bring to you my recent new step which has set me a *new goal, and that is when I decided to become a writer and an author. When I decided to become an author it has been three exciting years in the making at this point. I look back to when I started my business, and I could see that I loved expressing myself. Then one day I decided "Why not write a book, and have it published" well this idea came to me from the many friends that I have that wanted me to write a book. The more I thought about it, the more it made sense and* excited me. Well, I started my new venture by doing some research into the subject before I started. Boy was I in for a surprise in how many steps and how much time I would spend writing and publishing my book. I decided I am going for it, sink or swim "nothing ventured nothing gained" My writing career started with a science fiction novel called My Encounter, we are not Alone. A novel all about outer space, discoveries, and aliens, and you know my goal has become a reality. I now *write about many genus science fiction, children's stories, thrillers, westerns, romance, and horror stories. Although I realized there is still much more to learn.*

Dedication

I Michael Lee Kilmartin hereby dedicate my novels and short stories to my daughters Kristi and Lori. They inspired me to write my stories way back when they were just children. I can remember when I read my stories to them while taking a nap and at bedtime, how they became so excited when I read to them about aliens, and monsters that I had written for them.

About The Author

Michael did not come from a rich family; in fact, he came from a broken family at the age of six. Where his mother and father divorced, and the courts ordered Michael's Father and mother. Were ordered to have them sent to foster care. Michael and his brothers then were placed in several foster homes, and a boy's home for over six years, until their mother remarried in which Michael became an introverted shy child from the many places he was sent to as a child and making his

growing up years a nightmare and difficult

for him to talk to people.

From the Author

Hello everyone, my name is Michael Lee Kilmartin. I was born in the United States, and I am a native of California. I am a Scotsman and an Irishman. I grew up in a little town called Moorpark, California. My career for the last forty years has been as an entrepreneur, optimist, and philanthropist, and now an author with my company The Kilmartin Organization Inc.

\

AN

AUTHOR

IS

BORN

Contents

MICHAEL KILMARTIN BOOKS

MY CLOSE ENCOUNTER SERIES

SHORTY & SPARKY'S ADVENTURES

MY ENTREPRENEUR SERIES

BOOT HILL STORIES

FBI ASSIGNMENT SERIES

MICHAELS WAR STORIES

HALLOWEEN STORIES

MICHAEL SAY'S SERIES

MICHAELS WAR STORIES

MICHAELS HORROR STORIES

MEATBALLS SPACE SERIES

<u>MICHAEL KILMARTIN BOOKS</u>

MICHAELS LOVE STORIES

MICHAELS CHILDREN'S BOOKS

MICHAELS BABY BLUE SERIES

MICHAELS STEP-BY-STEP

TOMMY'S SPACE ADVENTURES

HOBBY'S SPACE ADVENTURES

STEPS TO MY SUCCESS SERIES

MICHAELS MY LIFE SERIES

MICHAEL THE AUTHOR IS BORN

MICHAELS ROMANCE SERIES

MICHAELS WOLF MAN SERIES

MICHAEL LEE KILMARTIN

AN AUTHOR IS BORN

Dedication

I Michael Lee Kilmartin hereby dedicate my novels and short stories to my daughters Kristi and Lori. They inspired me to write my stories way back when they were just children. I can remember when I read my stories to them while taking a nap and at bedtime, how they became so excited when I read to them about aliens, and monsters that I had written for them.

About The Author

Michael did not come from a rich family; in fact, he came from a broken family at the age of six. Where his mother and father divorced, and the courts ordered Michael's Father and mother. Were ordered to have them sent to foster care. Michael and his brothers then were placed in several foster homes, and a boy's home for over six years, until their mother remarried in which Michael became an introverted shy child from the many places he was sent to as a child and making his

growing up years a nightmare and difficult

for him to talk to people.

From the Author

Hello everyone, my name is Michael Lee Kilmartin. I was born in the United States, and I am a native of California. I am a Scotsman and an Irishman. I grew up in a little town called Moorpark, California. My career for the last forty years has been as an entrepreneur, optimist, and philanthropist, and now an author with my company The Kilmartin Organization Inc.

\

AN

AUTHOR

IS BORN

AN AUTHOR IS BORN

Chapter

1

My goal to become an author and it started back in 2017. My goal to be one has come true, and I am very happy that I decided to pursue my goal in writing.

Since I started I have written and published over 200 novels in children's stories, picture books, Western, science fiction, romance, thrillers, and horror stories.

I want my books to be perfect, and I continue to perfect my writing. I will never quit because success is in the air, and I can feel it.

Now I bring to you how I started and became an author with my new story and novel called "An Author is Born" One day *it came to me to write a book from the many comments to me by my friends and family "Michael you should become a writer, and an author"*

AN AUTHOR IS BORN

Chapter

2

The question was where and how I do I begin and start my new venture in writing, and I found that I would need to do some research to find out how. Including looking at the many authors that I have enjoyed following, Doctor Seuss, Jules Verne, George Lucas, Steven Spielberg, and many other fiction and nonfiction writers. and many professional people in business in how they got started. It is not like I have not written a story before. Because I have written many way back when I was in elementary and high school, and well into my college years.

I have always loved to write and express myself. I can write my stories in another time and place, and it has been an escape for me from many sad and hard times in my life. I found that could sit down and begin to write and be in any setting that I wanted to be in. It has been a total adventure for me. I do not claim to be a good writer, I want to be that great writer.

I still have a long way to go, but I will be there one day. Where people will then appreciate my writing and want to read more.

I will continue to practice and practice because I want to be a great writer. Where they will see and read my books and stories, and they will say, I have read and followed Michael Lee Kilmartin, and I have enjoyed reading his many novels,

and short stories, and his many books.

AN AUTHOR IS BORN

Chapter

3

I have found that it is not easy to be an

author, in fact it is hard work with many

long man-hours writing and studying my

manuscript and developing a new

manuscript.

But do you know "I love it" I have found that it is enjoyable for me, and educational.

I look back to when I first started and when I was just beginning. I could see now that my writing was not what I thought it should be. But do you know the more I would write the better that I felt about what I was writing "I am my worse critic"

I want my stories to be perfect just like painting a beautiful picture for all to see and would appreciate my writing? I began this new goal out of so many goals that I have created and accomplished. The more I would write the more I started to feel good about my writing.

I desperately at times wanted to feel like I was doing a good job of creating my stories and manuscripts. It is much like building my business the better I became at building my business, the better I would get.

I have always known the stories, and the ideas that I would write about, and that was step one for me. It was how to put my stories down on paper to make sense, which was the hard part. Even though the many things I have learned over my lifetime that I have created and developed in my business career.

AN AUTHOR IS BORN

Chapter

4

I will step back to mention a few things in my life that held me back and that was my past. I was an introvert, and I had a hard time talking to people which held me back from developing my vocabulary.

But when I started my business, I realized I needed to come out of the dark and bad dreams and begin to talk to people and discover life, and one day it came to me it was like turning on the light switch.

AN AUTHOR IS BORN

Chapter

5

Today I have no problem meeting people and discovering how I can help them and myself. I now can talk to people fluently, and I am finally not afraid to trust people.

I realized I needed more practice and more education in how to write. I can remember way back when I would read my stories, to my children and how they made me feel so good. I want that same feeling when people hear me talk and write.

I did not pursue writing as a career, I just wanted to explore the business, and yet I discovered that I love to write. I was just like everyone else making that almighty dollar, I have added it to my business as an ongoing way to express myself and to be able to create a new setting and a new world for me with my writing.

Here is something that I do remember at the beginning of my career "do what you love and make it a challenge to achieve success"

Truly if you want to be a great writer you need to love writing. I realized I needed to know how to create interesting paragraphs, spelling, and ending sentences, but most of all I needed an interesting story to write about and a topic to talk about, so that others will become interested in what I had to say in my writing.

Well, that is one thing I want to understand, until I went back to school to study English and Creative writing. I thought I could just sit down, and start writing whatever came to my mind, well it does not work that way.

I needed more education on how to structure the story and that takes years of education to find out how. Just in the last five years. I have taken many classes in college; creative writing, editing, critical thinking, sentence structure and even beginning writing and many more classes.

I found English History originated with the many writers of our past to build my writing career. The classes have been endless with the homework, and many hours spent in writing pages upon pages, and that the professors required. The professors would give the class three to *five topics to write on or about, some were interesting, and some were not so interesting critical thinking is one class I did not enjoy, but I did my best in trying to understand the topic.*

I would correct my writing over, and over in what I wrote about, which is ok until I felt like my work was now getting ready to be turned in for grading.

AN AUTHOR IS BORN

Chapter

6

Even to this day I rewrite and perfect my writing, as I am a perfectionist. The more I would write, the more I felt I was getting closer and closer to being a writer and an author.

My writing was now starting to make sense and started come together, with the many classes that I have taken and the many hours of practice in understanding how to write, and the importance to write a manuscript. I even went back to college, just to learn more about my other skills; Art, design, and illustration to perfect my book covers, and picture layouts in my books. It is worthwhile to do so if you plan on being a writer because the cover is the point of sale along with the description.

AN AUTHOR IS BORN

Chapter

7

I became even more excited in each step in my learning and yet I was still frustrated at times because my writing did not make sense to me.

I continue perfect my writing, drawing, and painting the more it was coming clearer to me in my mind what I was doing, but not completely in how to place my thoughts down on paper.

AN AUTHOR IS BORN

Chapter

8

The more I practiced, the more my skills advanced in each class and the more of the many steps I would need to understand, just like piecing together a puzzle. "Where does this go or does it go here" the more I would write and draw and paint the more it started to make sense in what I was writing.

I would write and publish my books and go back and edit and update my stories from time to time.

I realized that I needed to make the sentences and paragraphs more interesting. I found the key to a good sentence and paragraph is to make them interesting to read. I found that it is just like describing a beautiful place and painting a picture of how it should look.

I love to draw and paint. I have drawn many pictures over the years in my life that become useful in developing my books.

AN AUTHOR IS BORN

Chapter

9

My next step was to sit down and begin my manuscript of the story I was going to write about. I sat down to begin my first story and manuscript that I was going to write about, and I started to write an outline for a science fiction story "my favorite subject"

My first story in my mind and it goes like this. I wanted to write a science fiction story all about people and cultures from other worlds. I named my series "My Encounter, we are Not Alone" back in 2014.

I can remember way back in the fifties and sixties. I would go to the 5 and 10-cent stores and see the magazine stands to pick up a comic book that was all about aliens and outer space creatures.

I eventually had so many comic books, and stacks of them in my bedroom that it was wall to wall of them.

I used to watch a series called Flash Gordon and Star Trek each week on my TV. I watched them on a TV screen no bigger than ten inches in size, with another glass screen that was attached to the front for magnifying the picture.

I would watch Flash Gordon and the Star Trek series with spaceships, aliens, and strange worlds. I was glued to the set to watch both series. I was completely fascinated by the thought of being in space.

Even to this day, I am still fascinated by the subject of other life in space. I love going on the NASA website just to see where we are going with space travel.

We are definitely in a space race today "Amazing" With all countries and the many entrepreneurs getting in the act of space exploration.

Yes, I am a believer in other species in other worlds. Well, why not the universe it is teaming with thousands of worlds out there that can support life.

I certainly hope that I see that day when we do make contact with the first people of space "or have we already, I believe so"

I would say to myself when I watched both series "I sure wish I was born in that time, I would have loved to be a captain of a starship or just a traveler.

The more I watched science fiction stories and read my comics I wanted to know about outer space and the possibility of life on other planets.

I found that I was fascinated I would work and write for many hours well into the night just about outer space and aliens and extraterrestrials on other planets.

AN AUTHOR IS BORN

Chapter

10

I would set then set aside my manuscript and go onto another favorite series of mine called Shorty & Sparky's Adventures to write another story about them.

This is a children's series and a picture book series of mine with my two favorite animal dogs called Pugs and which I named Shorty and Sparky.

I have written many stories and picture books about them. Because I love animals. I have had five dogs, four Chihuahuas, and one French Bulldog ever since my daughters left home and went off to college in building their lives and career.

The oldest is Kristi who is 37, and she has my two granddaughters Harper and

Lucy, and another one on the way. Kristi moved from Long Beach just five years ago with her husband Tim to Cincinnati, Ohio where his family is. I got to see the oldest quite often while they lived in Long Beach.

It was a sad day for me when they moved because Kristi and her sister Lori were always with me and working in my business, until they went off to college, another sad day for me. Lori is close by, and I can still see her from time to time, she is 34 and still finding her way in life along with her career. I do not press her to find someone to settle down with, she has many friends, and I am proud of her.

AN AUTHOR IS BORN

Chapter

11

I love children and I love to write stories about children, and children's books, with pictures of all kinds of animals. When you are writing it is good to have another novel in progress to escape from one story and put yourself into another story.

Then you are fresh in your mind in what to continue with in your story. Having two novels in progress you can then relax into another world with two in progress. This way my mind does not get stagnant and off track when I do continue.

AN AUTHOR IS BORN

CHAPTER

12

Now in the beginning when I decided I was ready to publish, I had a choice to publish or self-publish. I chose self-publishing because it was much cheaper to self-publish than to publish with a publisher.

Granted your writing may not be perfect at first. but practice does make perfect and I always was changing my manuscript to read better.

Even though you get up to 100% of your royalties and their many fees that would be deducted from the 100%, in starting and editing.

Whereas in Self-publishing the publisher takes a large chunk of your royalties. This is OK in the beginning, because a little bit can add up to thousands, and they do not require you to buy large quantities of your books either.

Especially when you are first starting to write and publish your manuscripts and you have many changes, Some publishers will publish on demand, which means someone orders a book and the publisher makes and publishes the book from the original.

As I have said it is costly in the beginning, and there will be trial and error in your writing, and your covers you may decide to revise your edition over and over down the road. I have done this many times with my books until I felt good about what I have written and published, and usually, the second or third time around, which is many more hours of my time.

I am my worst critic when it comes to my books and my stories and my cover designs. But that is OK, I am still in the learning stage in writing.

Until I begin to enjoy and start to publish more and more of my stories. Then

I can decide to change to a publisher that will supply you with an editor and cover designer at a cost. Unless you are like me and you know how to draw and paint, and you have an eye for design. You can see how the cover should look in your story and your mind, and how others will see it.

Good computer skills are vital as knowing how to use computer tools. I was not at first good at using the computer, but practice does make perfect. I enjoy trying new things all the time with the tools and programs that are available today. I have Adobe Illustrator for producing my book covers, where you can design a creative design for your book. Although it takes many hours in discovering the tools how to set up your layout, and design.

AN AUTHOR IS BORN

CHAPTER

13

Computer tools are endless, like using adobe Illustrator, what a nightmare, and until I learned the tools, I can now make beautiful pictures and designs.

Having a good word program is vital as well as it corrects your spelling when you are writing your manuscript.

Some publishers do inform you that a word here and there is misspelled when it is ready.

This is very important, especially when you publish your first book, and you see errors in many parts of your book. "How embarrassing is that" I have been there and done that, and I am still correcting my work and that is OK as long as I am learning and seeing my mistakes. In the final stages of publishing, I begin to market my book. I do not want to be surprised when I find that is book is not selling.

I then realize I am in a pool of millions of books being sold out there with millions of readers and writers.

I marketing my name is very important so that they can remember me, and they can find my boo with many retailers. You can market and advertise your books in their stores and on their websites. Another

way is to sell your book as a Kindle book,

and that is where you can sell your book

to customers just by reading them online,

and you can receive royalties when they

read each page. Digital is the wave of the

future.

Most publishers have this now, and

many will place your books with Barnes

and Noble, Amazon, and many other

websites. Just look up an author on

Google and you will see the many places

where their books are being published on their websites. Another way is to find a sales rep company in your area that will sell your book or books door to door to libraries, and stores near where you live, and out of the area for a commission.

I have been doing this personally and I have even gone out with them to sell my books to the bookstores and libraries, and to introduce myself to the owners and managers of the stores, including doing a book signing in the stores.

Get your books out there in every way you can. I have even seen some authors take their books to flea markets and sell them "Be a peddler" meaning a salesperson until you are successful with your name and books. There are so many outlets out there to sell your books on that will advertise them; Twitter, Facebook, and Instagram. I find Facebook an excellent way to get your books out there in the public's eyes. Have you ever seen how many are on Facebook and Twitter.

"Exposure is the key"

Happy writing e eryone and maybe

you will be the next bestseller and

author on the "New York Best Sellers

List"

Good Luck

Everyone

The End

www.ingramcontent.com/pod-product-compliance
Lightning Source LLC
Chambersburg PA
CBHW070429180526
45158CB00017B/934